THE GREAT COMPOSERS FAKEBOOK

Compiled and arranged by James H. Bryan

AMSCO PUBLICATIONS
NEW YORK • LONDON • PARIS • SYDNEY

Order No. AM 948827
US International Standard Book Number: 0.8256.1702.2
UK International Standard Book Number: 0.7119.7601.5

Exclusive Distributors:
MUSIC SALES CORPORATION
257 Park Avenue South, New York, NY 10010 USA
MUSIC SALES LIMITED
8/9 Frith Street, London W1D 3JB England
MUSIC SALES PTY. LIMITED
120 Rothschild Street, Rosebery, Sydney, NSW 2018, Australia

Printed in the United States of America by
Vicks Lithograph and Printing Corporation

CONTENTS

INTRODUCTION

These famous melodies were chosen for their beauty and practicality. Many well-known pieces uncommon to this type of book have been included here in the hope that this volume will be used beyond the living room and teaching studio. Accompanied by a keyboard or guitar, many of these selections will be appropriate in wedding ceremonies, lounges, and in the park.

PERFORMANCE TIPS

Suggested tempos have been indicated by metronome markings.

Violinists and flutists may prefer to play some passages up an octave.

Recorder players have been given a few alternate notes where range may be a problem. Although notes above high D on the soprano recorder can be attained through experimentation with alternate fingerings, the judicious player may prefer octave displacement in many cases.

Each duet may also be played as a solo. Accompanists should be aware that the second parts are not necessarily bass lines.

EXPLANATION OF CHORD SYMBOLS

Symbol	chord notes	description
N.C.		No Chord
C bass	C	No Chord with a C note in the bass
C	C E G	C Major
C/E	E C G	C Major with an E note in the bass
Cm	C E♭ G	C Minor
Cm6	C E♭ G A	C Minor Sixth
Cm7	C E♭ G B♭	C Minor Seventh
Cm(maj7)	C E♭ G B	C Minor with a Major Seventh
C°	C E♭ G♭	C Diminished
C+	C E G♯	C Augmented
C6	C E G A	C Major Sixth
C7	C E G B♭	C Dominant Seventh
C7♭9	C E G B♭ D♭	C Dominant Seventh Flatted Ninth
Cmaj7	C E G B	C Major Seventh
Cmaj7♯5	C E G♯ B	C Major Seventh Sharped Fifth
C9	C E G B♭ D	C Dominant Ninth
Cø7 or Cm7♭5	C E♭ G♭ B♭	C Half-Diminished Seventh (C Minor Seventh Flatted Fifth)
C°7	C E♭ G♭ B♭♭	C Diminished Seventh
Cadd ♯11	C E G F♯	C Major with a Sharped Eleventh
C5	C G	C with no third

Symbol	chord notes	description
C (no 5)	C E	C with no fifth
C6 (no 3)	C G A	C Major Sixth with no third
C7 (no 3)	C G B♭	C Dominant Seventh with no third
C7 (no 5)	C E B♭	C Dominant Seventh with no fifth
Csus4	C F G	C Suspended Fourth
Csus2	C D G	C Suspended Second
C$^{sus4}_{sus2}$	C D F G	C Suspended Second and Fourth
C7sus4	C F G B♭	C Dominant Seventh Suspended Fourth

TRANSPOSING

Musicians who play transposing instruments can play any tune in this book as written if unaccompanied. If accompanied, selections must be transposed as follows:

B♭ Instruments   (Clarinet, Trumpet, Tenor Saxophone)   up a major 2nd
(or up a major 9th if desired).

E♭ Instruments   (Alto Saxophone)   up a major 6th.

TRANSPOSITION EXAMPLES

Change the note and key signature as indicated:

	B♭	E♭
If the instrument is pitched in:		
A C note and the key signature in C become:	D	A

If you want to play the tunes in this book as written on your transposing instrument, your accompanist should transpose the chords and key signature down by the appropriate interval.

ABOUT THE AUTHOR

James H. Bryan grew up on a farm near Wingate, Texas. Following high school, he served as a trumpeter in the 745th and 535th United States Air Force bands. In 1969 he earned a Bachelor of Music degree at the University of Texas at Austin with a major in Music Literature. He received a Master of Music in Orchestral Conducting from Arizona State University in 1972 and currently is a music merchant and performer in Austin, Texas.

FORLANA

Jacques Aubert

Tango in D

Isaac Albéniz

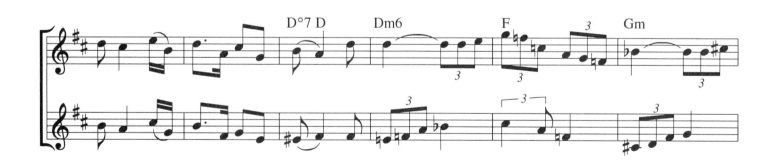

Air
from Orchestral Suite No. 3

Johann Sebastian Bach

Arioso

Johann Sebastian Bach

Ave Maria

J.S. Bach/Charles Gounod

Bourée

from Cello Suite No. 3

Johann Sebastian Bach

Minuet
from Orchestral Suite No. 2

Johann Sebastian Bach

Badinerie
from Orchestral Suite No. 2

Johann Sebastian Bach

Jesu, Joy of Man's Desiring
from Cantata No. 147

Johann Sebastian Bach

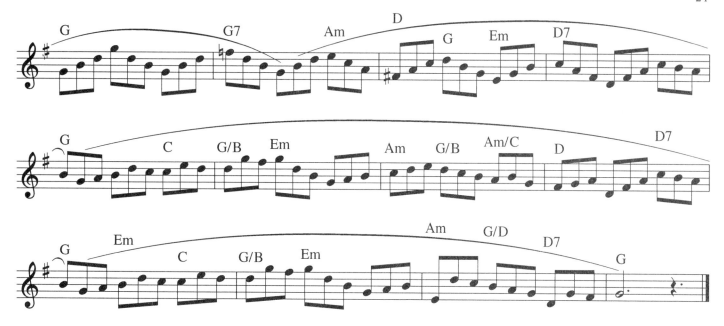

Minuet in G

Johann Sebastian Bach

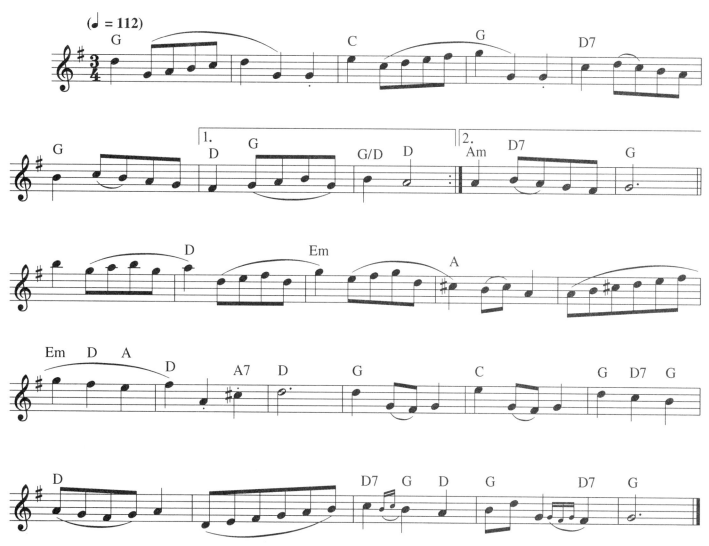

Rondo—Gavotte
from Violin Partita No. 3

Johann Sebastian Bach

Sleepers, Awake!

"Wachet Auf!" from Cantata No. 140

Johann Sebastian Bach

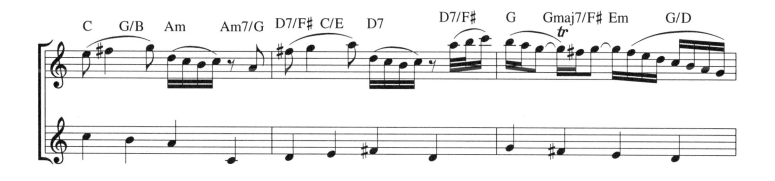

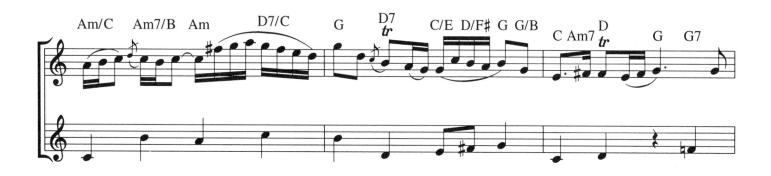

Für Elise

Ludwig van Beethoven

Minuet in G

Ludwig van Beethoven

Rage over a Lost Penny
(Rondo a Capriccio)

Ludwig van Beethoven

Andante
from Symphony No. 5

Ludwig van Beethoven

Symphony No. 6
(Theme from Second Movement)

Ludwig van Beethoven

ODE TO JOY
from Symphony No. 9

Ludwig van Beethoven

both parts in unison or octaves

Turkish March

Ludwig van Beethoven

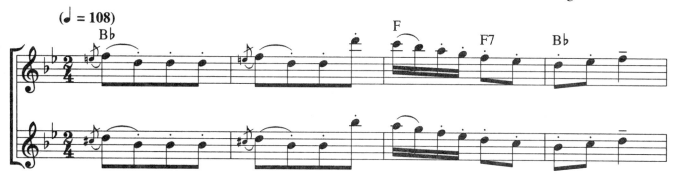

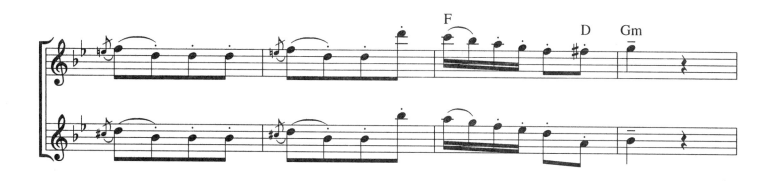

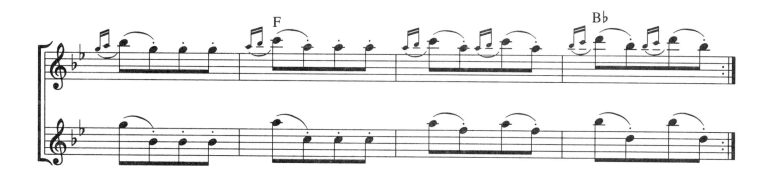

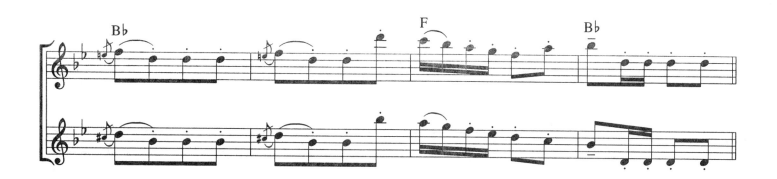

Rákoczy March

Hector Berlioz

Changing of the Guard
from Carmen

Georges Bizet

HABANERA
from Carmen

Georges Bizet

ENTR'ACTE TO ACT II
from Carmen

Georges Bizet

ENTR'ACTE TO ACT III
from Carmen

Georges Bizet

Farandole
from L'Arlésienne Suite No. 2

Georges Bizet

Serenade
from The Pearl Fishers

Georges Bizet

Minuet

Luigi Boccherini

Nocturne
from String Quartet No. 2

Alexander Borodin

Polovtsian Dance
from Prince Igor

Alexander Borodin

CRADLE SONG

Johannes Brahms

GAUDEAMUS IGITUR
from Academic Festival Overture

Johannes Brahms

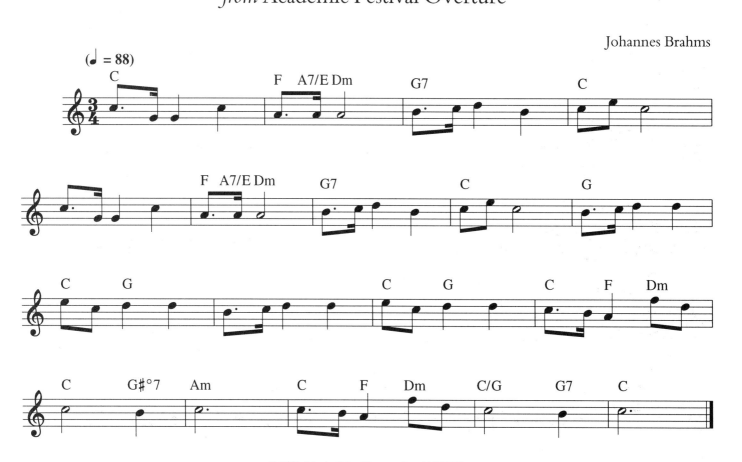

Variations on a Theme by Haydn

Johannes Brahms

Variation No.7

Hungarian Dance No. 5

Johannes Brahms

Symphony No. 1
(Theme from Fourth Movement)

Johannes Brahms

Waltz in A-Flat
(Op. 39, No. 15)

Johannes Brahms

CHOPIN MEDLEY
Etude *(Op. 10, No. 3)*, Fantasie-Impromptu *(Op. 66)*, Nocturne *(Op. 9, No. 2)*

Frédéric Chopin

Prelude
(Op. 28, No. 4)

Frédéric Chopin

Prelude
(Op. 28, No. 7)

Frédéric Chopin

Minute Waltz
(Op. 64, No. 1)

Frédéric Chopin

Waltz
(Op. 64, No. 2)

Frédéric Chopin

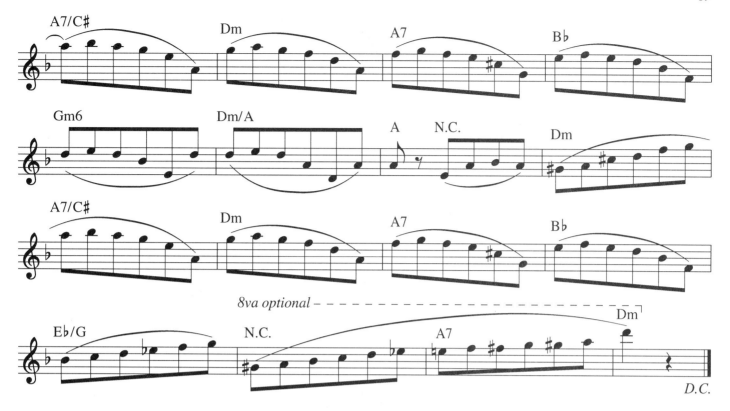

TRUMPET VOLUNTARY

Jeremiah Clarke

Sonata No. 1

Muzio Clementi

Pizzicati

From Sylvia

Léo Delibes

D.S. al Fine

Valse Lente
from Coppélia

Léo Delibes

Chopsticks

Arthur de Lulli

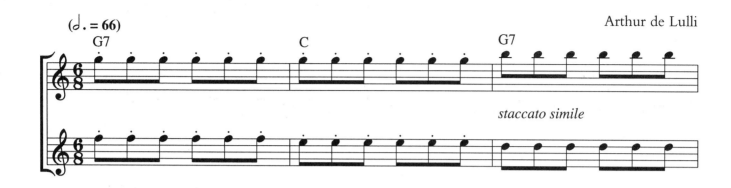

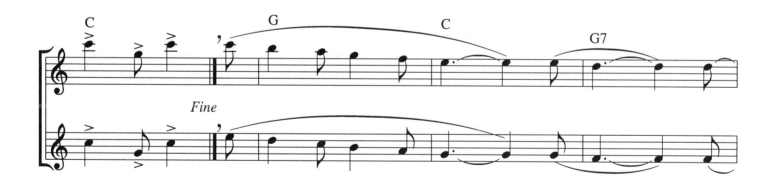

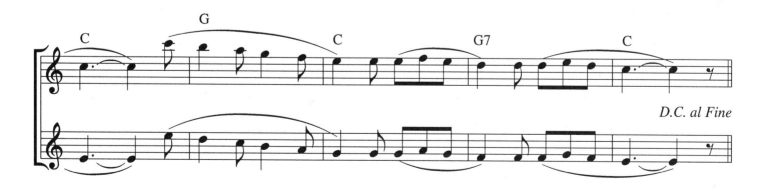

O Sole Mio

Eduardo Di Capua

Sextet
from Lucia di Lammermoor

Gaetano Donizetti

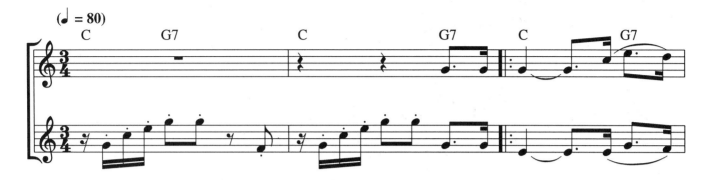

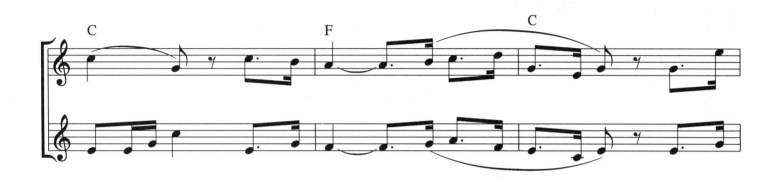

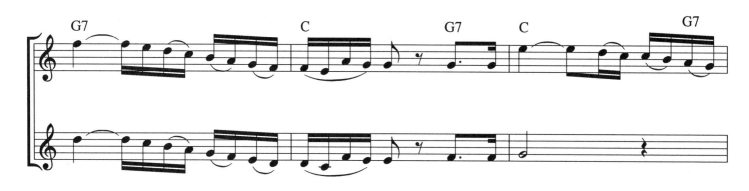

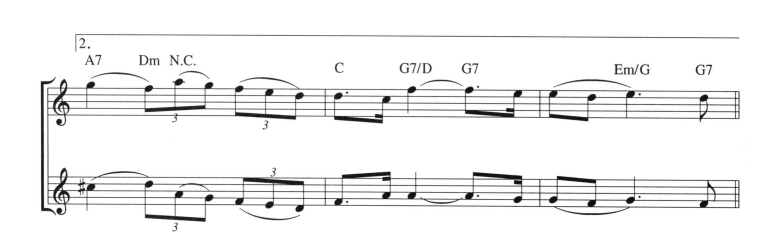

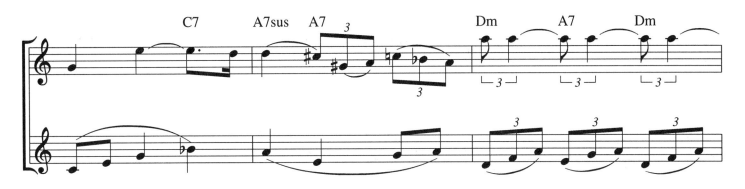

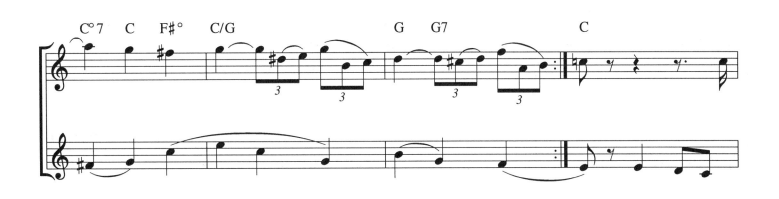

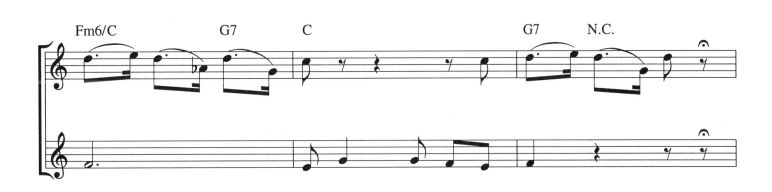

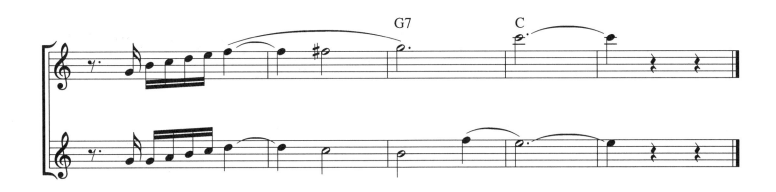

DVOŘÁK MEDLEY
Songs My Mother Taught Me, Largo *from* New World Symphony

Songs My Mother Taught Me

Antonín Dvořák

Humoresque

Antonín Dvořák

Fine

D.S. al Fine

The New Sa-Hoo

Giles Farnaby

A Toye

Giles Farnaby

AH! SO PURE
from Martha

Frederich von Flotow

Rustic Wedding

Carl Goldmark

Tambourin

François Joseph Gossec

Funeral March of a Marionette

Charles Gounod

Spanish Dance No. 5
"Playera"

Enríque Granados

MORNING
from Peer Gynt

Edvard Grieg

Anitra's Dance
from Peer Gynt

Edvard Grieg

I Know That My Redeemer Liveth

from Messiah

George Frideric Handel

Overture and Minuet II
from Music for the Royal Fireworks

George Frideric Handel

See, the Conquering Hero Comes

from Judas Maccabæus

George Frideric Handel

Air
from Water Music

George Frideric Handel

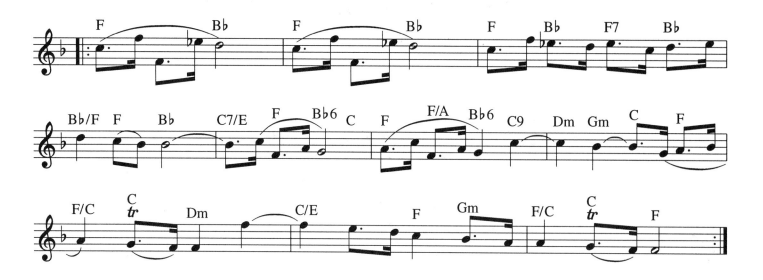

Bourée
from Water Music

George Frideric Handel

ALLEGRO DECISO—FINALE

from Water Music

George Frideric Handel

Serenade
from String Quartet *(Op. 3, No. 5)*

Franz Joseph Haydn

Lullaby
from Hänsel and Gretel

Engelbert Humperdinck

Procession of the Sardar
from Caucasian Sketches

Mikhail Ippolitov-Ivanov

Parade of the Wooden Soldiers

Leon Jessel

Pastorale

Jean T. Latour

Hungarian Rhapsody No. 2

Franz Liszt

ADAGIO

Alessandro Marcello

THE GOLDEN WEDDING
"La cinquantaine"

Gabriel Marie

Fine

D.S. al Fine

Aragonaise
from Le Cid

Jules Massenet

To a Wild Rose

Edward MacDowell

Meditation
from Thaïs

Jules Massenet

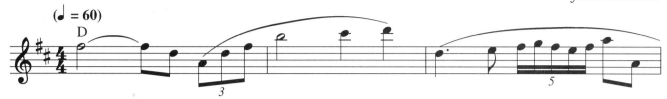

Nocturne
from A Midsummer Night's Dream

Felix Mendelssohn

Wedding March
from A Midsummer Night's Dream

Felix Mendelssohn

Coronation March

Giacomo Meyerbeer

Pictures at an Exhibition

Modest Mussorgsky

Promenade I

attacca

The Old Castle

attacca

128

Promenade II

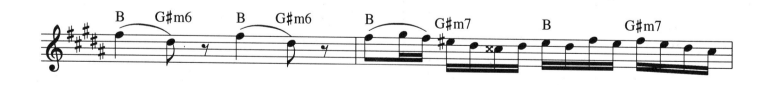

attacca

Tuileries (Children Quarreling after Play)

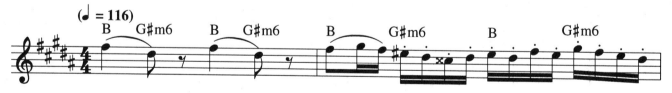

attacca

Bydlo (The Oxcart)

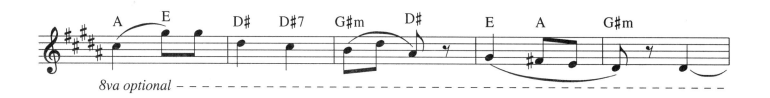

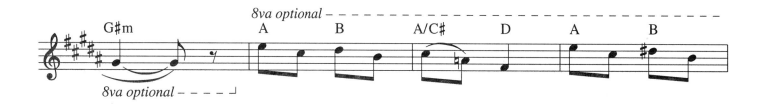

attacca

The Great Gate of Kiev

8va optional

Piano Concerto No. 21
(Theme from Second Movement)

Wolfgang Amadeus Mozart

Romance
from Eine Kleine Nachtmusik

Wolfgang Amadeus Mozart

Menuetto
from Eine Kleine Nachtmusik

Wolfgang Amadeus Mozart

LA CI DAREM LA MANO
"Give Me Your Hand" from Don Giovanni

Wolfgang Amadeus Mozart

Non più andrai, farfallone amoroso

"Say Goodbye Now to Pastime" from The Marriage of Figaro

Wolfgang Amadeus Mozart

Piano Concerto No. 20
(Theme from Second Movement)

Wolfgang Amadeus Mozart

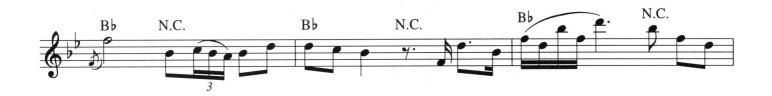

Andante
from Sonata No. 11

Wolfgang Amadeus Mozart

Rondo alla Turca
from Sonata No. 11

Wolfgang Amadeus Mozart

Sonata No. 16

(Theme from First Movement)

Wolfgang Amadeus Mozart

Can Can

Jacques Offenbach

Waltz in C

Ignaz Joseph Pleyel

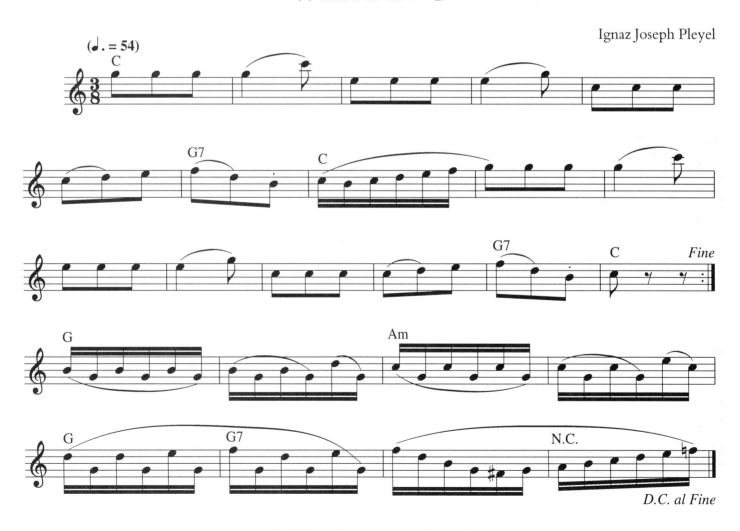

Dance of the Hours
from La Gioconda

Amilcare Ponchielli

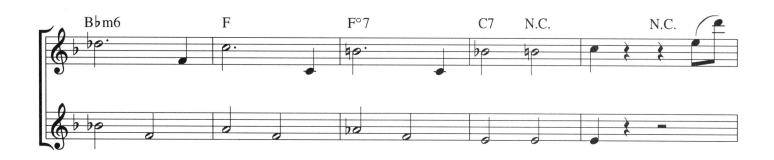

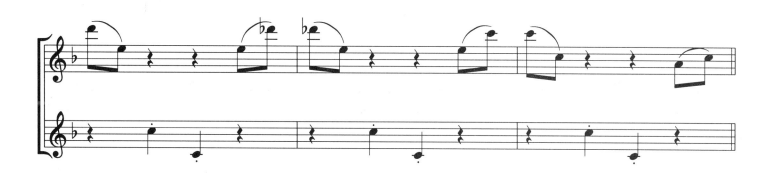

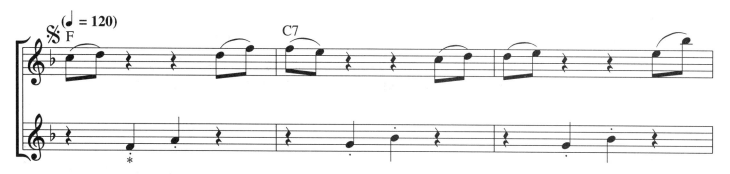

* For a special effect, substitute a duck call (or similar noisemaker) here.

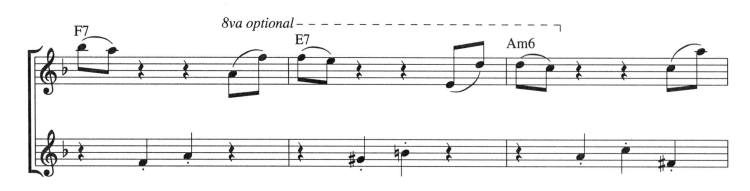

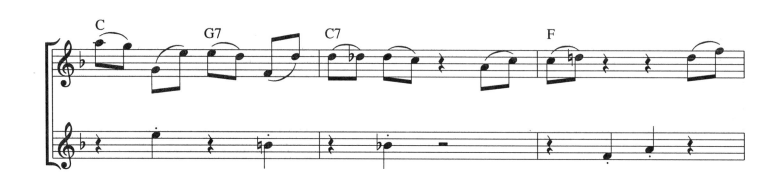

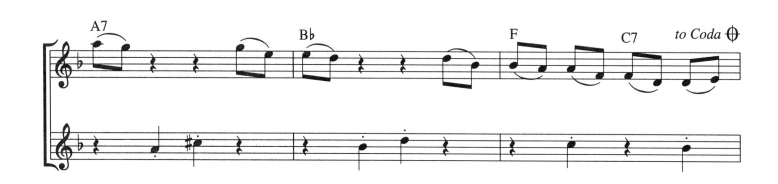

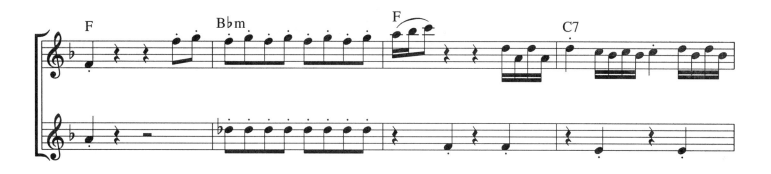

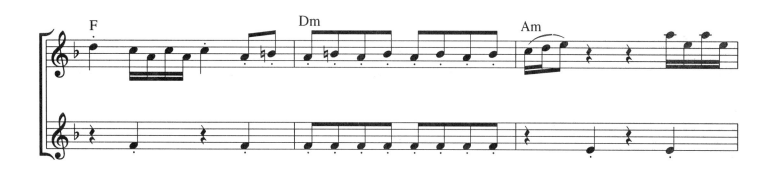

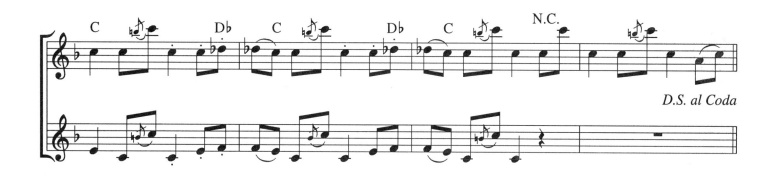

D.S. al Coda

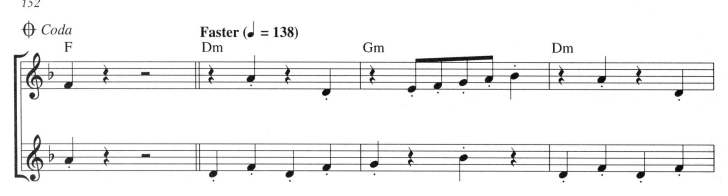

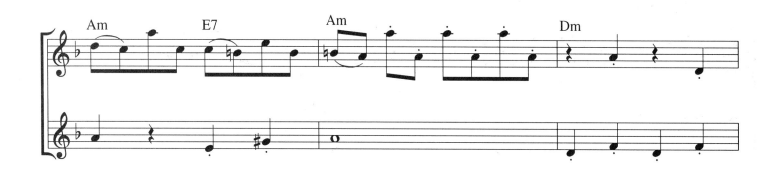

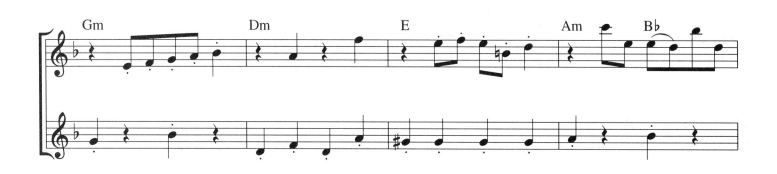

Musetta's Waltz Song
from La Bohème

Giacomo Puccini

O MIO BABBINO CARO

"My Dear Father" from Gianni Schicchi

Giacomo Puccini

Festival Rondo
from Abdelazar

Henry Purcell

D.C. al Fine

TRUMPET TUNE

Henry Purcell

Tambourin

Jean-Philippe Rameau

MENEUT EN RONDEAU

Jean-Philippe Rameau

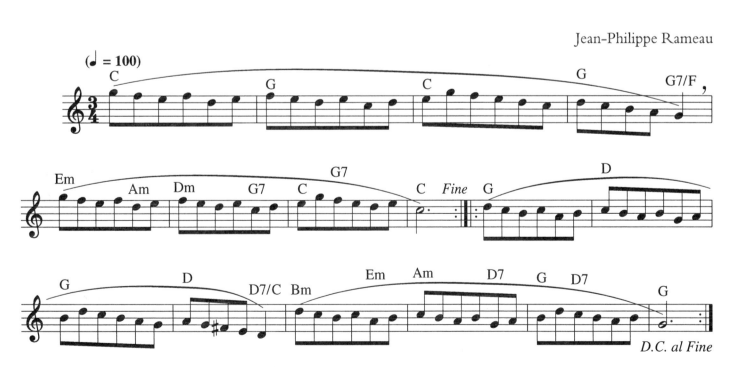

RIMSKY-KORSAKOV MEDLEY
Hymn to the Sun, Song of India

Nikolai Rimsky-Korsakov

Song of India

Scheherazade

Nikolai Rimsky-Korsakov

William Tell Overture

Gioacchino Rossini

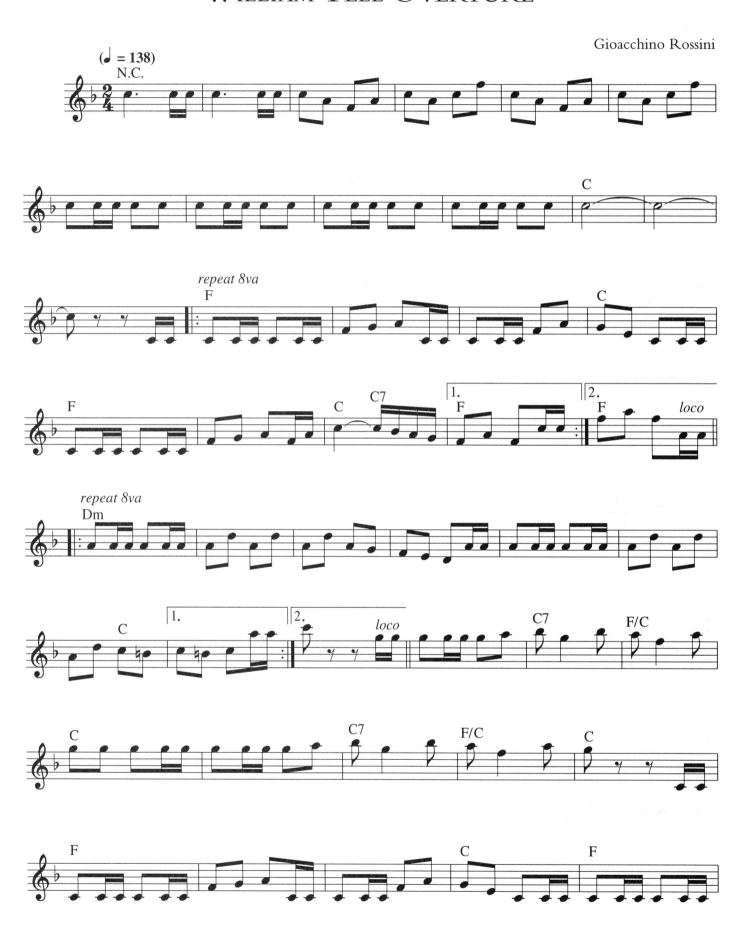

GYMNOPÉDIE No. 1

Erik Satie

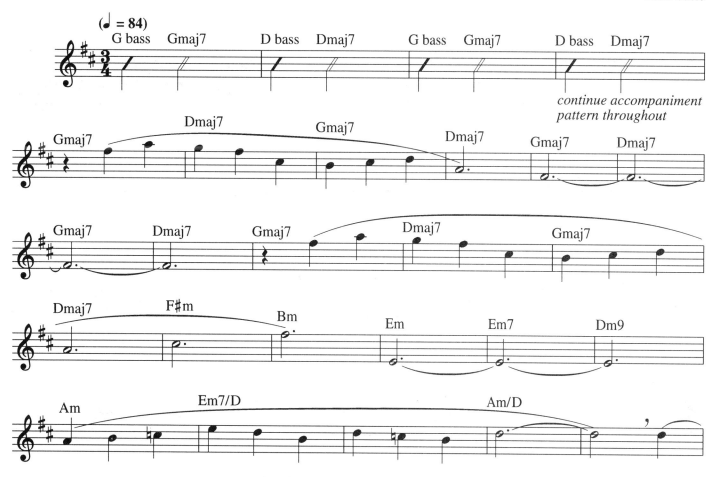

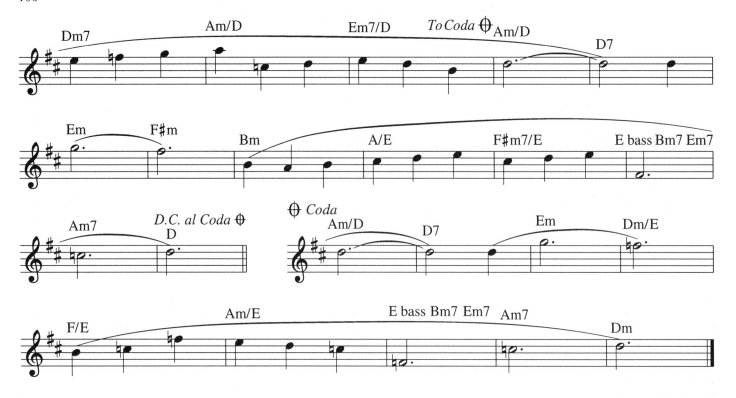

AVE MARIA

Franz Schubert

THE HAPPY FARMER

Robert Schumann

Moment Musicale

Franz Schubert

Sonata in C
(L. 104)

Domenico Scarlatti

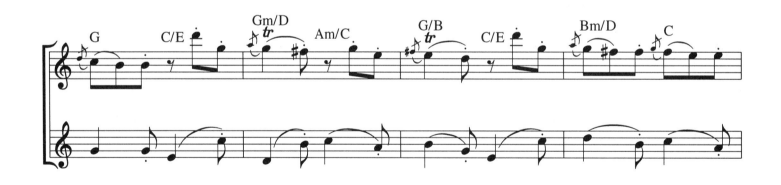

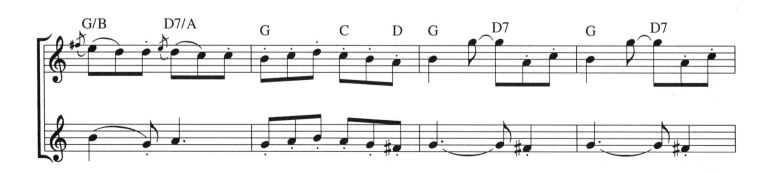

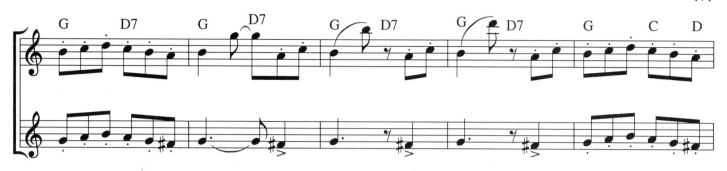

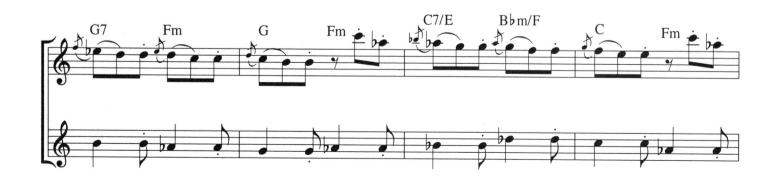

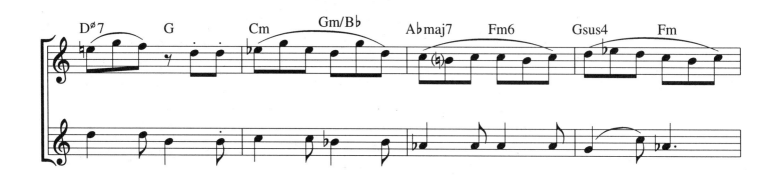

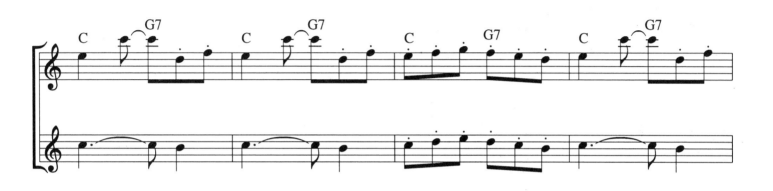

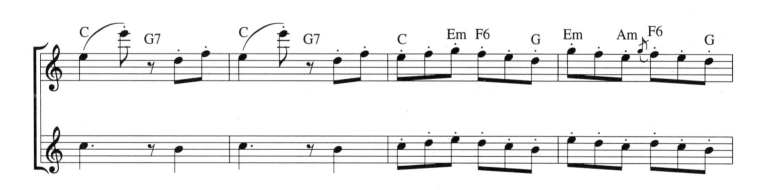

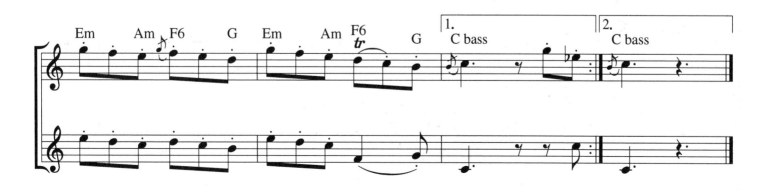

Sonata in D Minor
(L. 413)

Domenico Scarlatti

The Stars and Stripes Forever

John Philip Sousa

Piccolo solo ad lib.

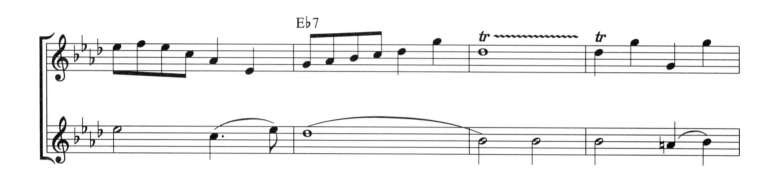

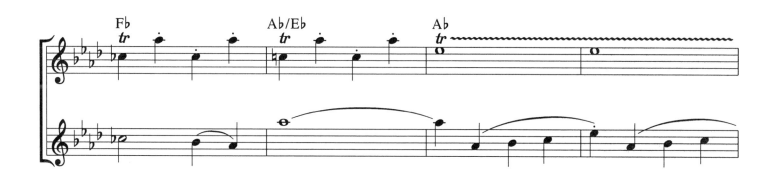

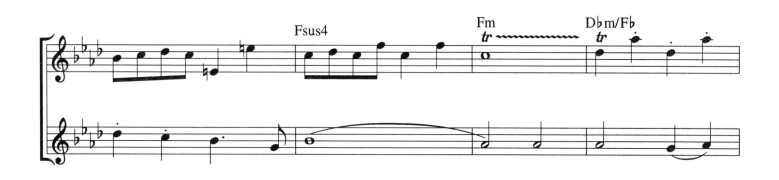

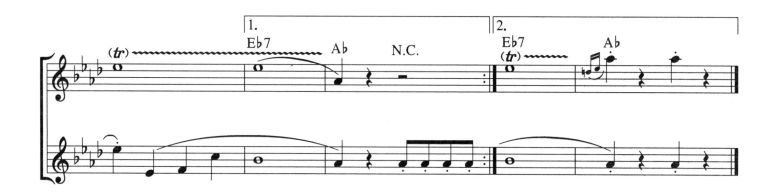

On the Beautiful Blue Danube

Johann Strauss

Radetsky March

Johann Strauss

Roses from the South

Johann Strauss

You and You

from Die Fledermaus

Johann Strauss

Dance of the Sugarplum Fairy
from The Nutcracker

Peter Ilyich Tchaikovsky

Russian Dance
from The Nutcracker

Peter Ilyich Tchaikovsky

DANCE OF THE REED FLUTES
from The Nutcracker

Peter Ilyich Tchaikovsky

Waltz of the Flowers
from The Nutcracker

Peter Ilyich Tchaikovsky

June
Barcarolle

Peter Ilyich Tchaikovsky

Russian March Medley
March Slav, Russian Sailors' Dance

Peter Ilyich Tchaikovsky/Anonymous

Swan Lake
(Theme)

Peter Ilyich Tchaikovsky

Swan Lake Medley
Dance of the Swans, Danse Napolitaine

Peter Ilyich Tchaikovsky

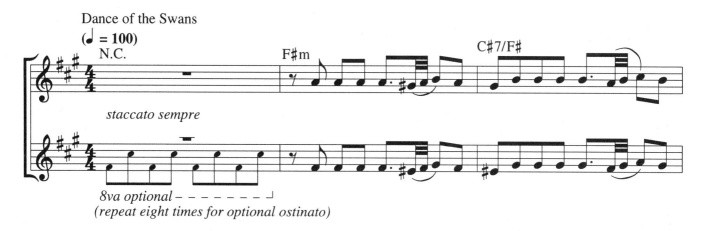

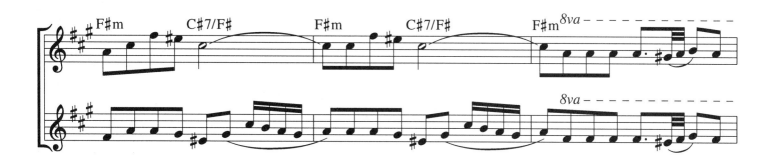

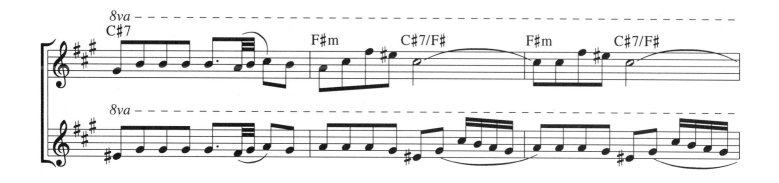

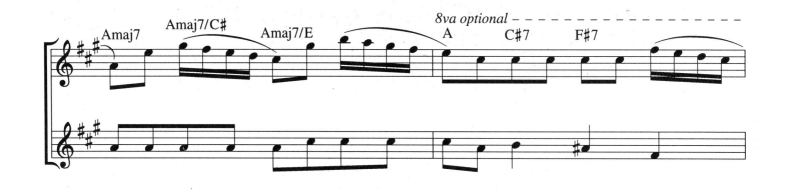

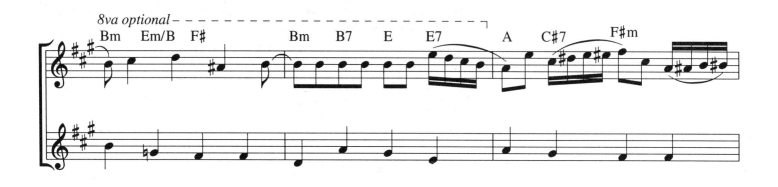

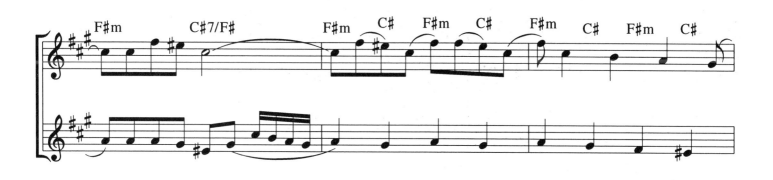

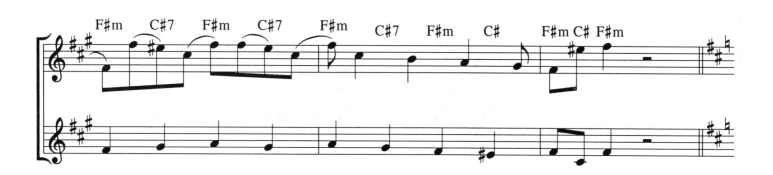

Danse Napolitaine

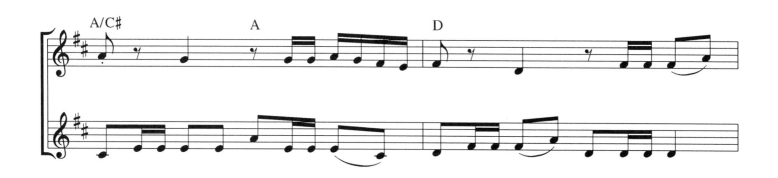

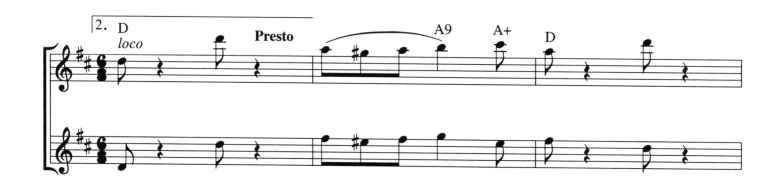

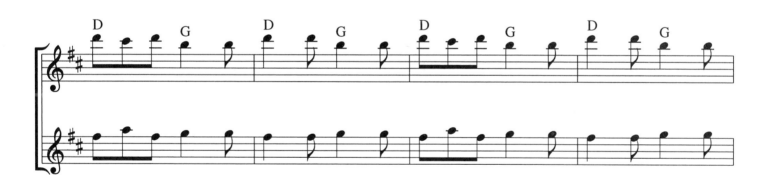

Symphony No. 5
(Theme from Second Movement)

Peter Ilyich Tchaikovsky

SYMPHONY No. 6
"Pathétique" *(Theme from First Movement)*

Peter Ilyich Tchaikovsky

Waltz
from Serenade for Strings

Peter Ilyich Tchaikovsky

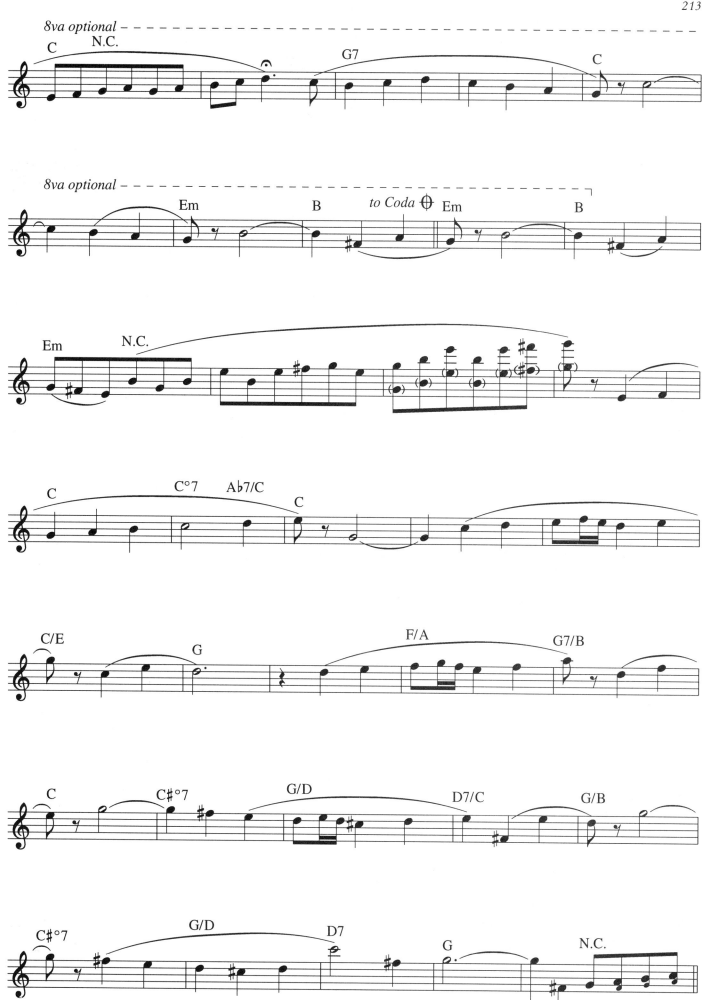

TÜRK MEDLEY
Hunting Horns and Echo, Arioso, March

Daniel Gottlieb Türk

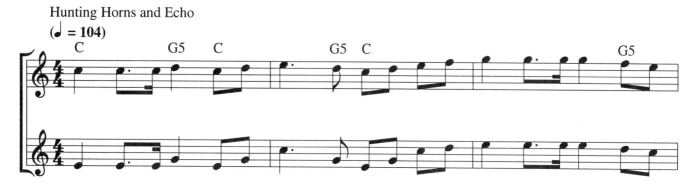

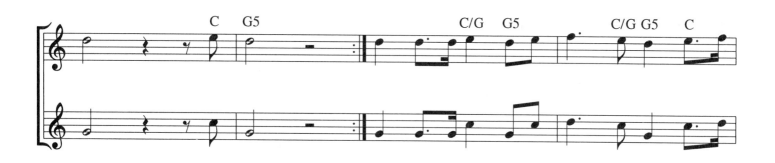

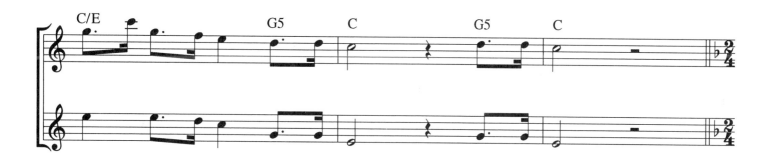

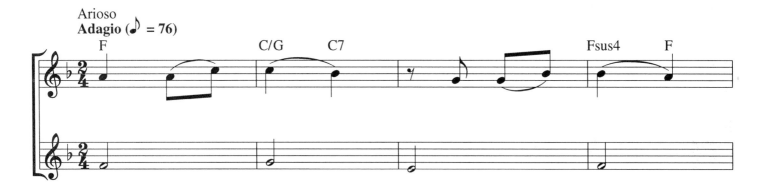

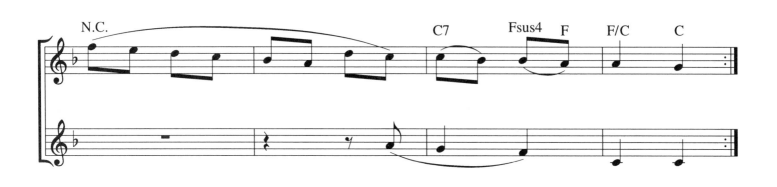

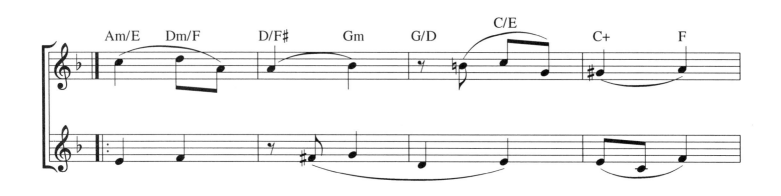

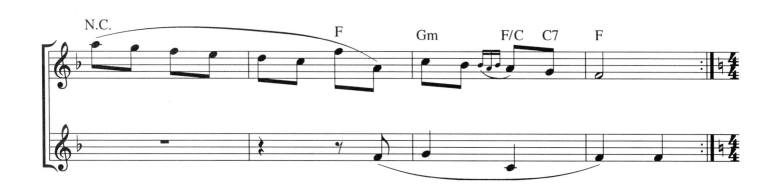

March
(♩ = 108)

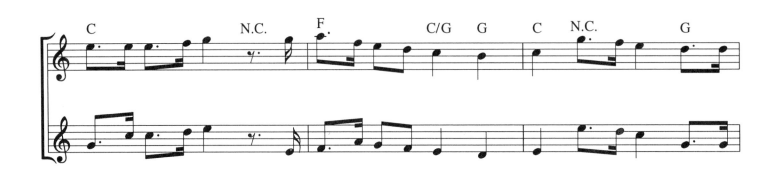

CARO NOME
"Dearest Name" from Rigoletto

Giuseppe Verdi

GRAND MARCH
from Aïda

Giueppe Verdi

Under the Double Eagle

Joseph Wagner

D.C. al Fine

Bridal Chorus
from Lohengrin

Richard Wagner

España Waltzes

Emil Waldteufel

D.C. al Fine

The Skaters Waltz

Emil Waldteufel

Unter Der Linden

Walter von der Vogelweide

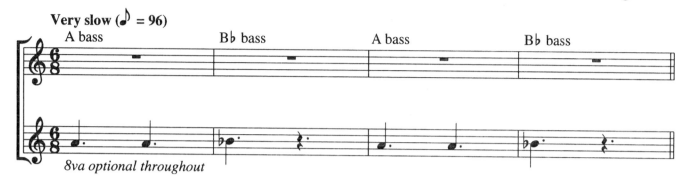

Agniau Dous

Anonymous

THE BRITISH GRENADIERS

Anonymous

COUNTRY GARDENS

Anonymous

DELIGHTFUL DIRGE MEDLEY
Dies Irae, Volga Boatmen Song, Funeral March

Anonymous/Chopin

Dona Nobis Pacem
Three-Part Round

Anonymous

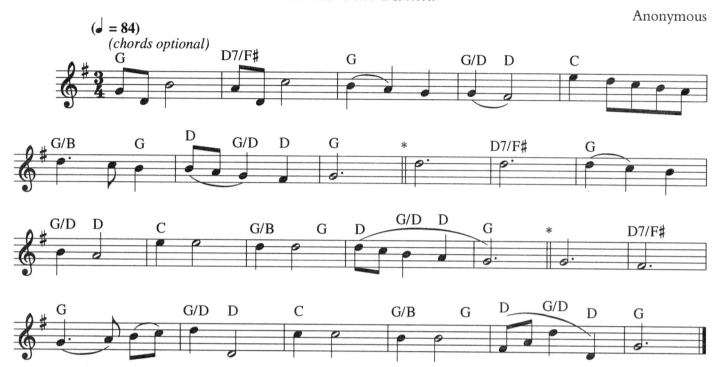

* entrance points for additional voices

Galliard

Anonymous

Jouyssance vous donnerai

Burgundian Basse Dance

Anonymous

Fine

unison, first time;
both parts, second time

D.C. and repeat ad lib.

THREE EARLY POPULAR SONGS
Winter Is Past, En Mai la rousée, Simple Gifts

Anonymous

Simple Gifts

LILLIBURLERO

Anonymous

SUMER IS ICUMEN IN

Four-Part Round

Anonymous

* entrance points for additional voices